Wisdom at Work

30 Days to Better Management

A H Fleming

Contents

Wisdom at Work

2012 Max Life Book Series

Published by
Creative Media Concepts

Ayub H. Fleming, Author

Introduction

I wanted to share with you over 20 years of management experience and the lessons that I have learned along the way. If you read one lesson a day and apply that lesson you will strengthen your management skills and increase your ability to get your staff motivated and more efficient. One of the hardest things to do is manage people. It has to be done and done well because people are by far your greatest asset. The management of persons and the development of good systems will make or break any business.

This is not an educational course. Its life lessons learned from experience that can help you develop a management philosophy for any business. Why is a management philosophy important, because philosophy is where everything starts? It's the belief system that gives to the reason why and the explanation of how. Systems make management philosophies practical down to everyday policy and procedure for the work to be done.

Human nature requires having a reason why we do things. To not have an underlying philosophy is to do things disconnected from purpose. If you do that then you are bound to fail sooner or later. The support of the right product in the right market will fail if you don't understand how and why you are doing what you are doing.

By reading and applying one lesson a day you can become a better manager in 30 days.

Chapter 1

There is no I in TEAM, but there is one in WIN

Teamwork is the ability to work together toward a common vision. The ability to direct individual accomplishments toward organizational objectives. It is the fuel that allows common people to attain uncommon results.

Henry Ford

There has been so much written about teamwork and how to build great teams. Many have studied the examples of great business models and athletic teams who achieved greatness as well as many recounting their experience being on successful teams.

Everyday as leaders, managers, and even team players we ask ourselves, how do we win? How do we achieve our objectives? Our focus is to build better teams because we have to work together to win. Without the incentive to win or a clear objective on what winning looks like we have simply a herd moving loosely in the same direction with differing visions and hardly ever if at any time the same mission.

I have been on some horrible management teams that accomplished little as a team but we were great as individual achievers. The typical consultant was brought in to build trust and team building exercises that did little more than to fuel our determination to be individuals that much more. Because we were top-level managers our competitive nature would not let us focus on team, but rather on achievement. It happened that no one was looking at the big picture and noticed that we accomplished a great deal though we never learned to trust each other. How much more could we have accomplished if we really worked together toward a common goal.

The company at the time hired a high paid consultant to come in to lead us in exercises and role-playing in developing teamwork and trust. The Directors in the company at the time were very territorial and were not about to lower their guard in order to practice some new hand holding excising and singing among the lilies. We individually were stars and we wanted the last shot, we only passed the ball and supported the other when it was necessary. We did not dislike each other but there was always tension sometimes that undermined the projects due to lack of communication and trust.

I remember the first few meetings with the consultant. It seemed that as we met no one wanted to talk much less be there. The tension became so great that everyone was so determined to do their own thing that the project was scrapped.

Does lack of communication make projects suffer and untold waste of money time and resources in business? Absolutely it does. There was a lot of duplication of work much of it caused by the owner telling more than one person to do to the same job and instead of passing off the task to the person responsible they would pursue doing it themselves. Daily wars erupted.

I believe a generation ago, teamwork was easier because earlier generations believed in pulling together to fight the common enemy or to achieve the common goal. Individuality was not the mantra of the day until the 60's and 70's where individual voices that raged against the machine were heard with great upheaval.

If you want to be a successful team builder today you have to understand that individuals have different values than previous generations. It's not better or worse per say, just different.

Today there is an I in team. With over 20 years of management experience including construction and other disciplines, I have noticed a distinct difference in the attitudes of people recently toward team building and working together. In sports today, a brand is created many times before the individuals or even the success of the team. Many super stars in basketball play for teams who in their career have never won a championship but are touted for their individual play rather than the team achievement. It's a rare athlete today who is willing to pay the price for success and sacrifice for the team for the championship and not just the shoe deal or the larger salary.

Individuality in teams and creating stars among them is what society is beginning to produce. Economics also makes working for one company throughout your career and into retirement years is nearly impossible anymore. People are not just switching companies they are having 2 and 3 careers within one working lifetime.

The age of free agency is here and its here to stay. The age of technology and the ease of information, developing information and distributing it is making people seek other alternatives and ways of looking at careers and loyalty to companies.

So to understand team building today you have to mix old school principles with new school values and points of view to create a new paradigm that works for today's business and team building.

1. **The team is both made up of individuals and the team as a whole.**

Today's leaders who have to build teams to achieve a specific goal must not seek to build a homogenized unit that looks and thinks the same. There is no real benefit to consensus style of management if all avenues and possibilities have not been explored.

There is a real benefit to individuals disagreeing in a manner where all avenues of "how to" are explored. The days of top level management meeting and making decisions without input from all levels of employees from creators, management and people doing the tasks should be over. Companies no matter how large or small have to see themselves as more entrepreneurial in nature developing input and synergy from suppliers and other strategic partners. Developing the mastermind alliance between divisions or departments should be the new business model for achievement.

Many things create synergy on the surface even though sometimes contradiction is going on beneath the surface. Major disagreements can grow out of minor ones when there is no open forum or system for the individual to be heard. When an individual grows frustrated and feels they have no safe place in which to express themselves they will either contribute nothing beyond the task assigned to them or undermine the process from the beginning.

The manager today must remember and actually plan for both team and individual achievement and recognition. To achieve this, the leader must first establish a goal for the team to achieve. A clearly defined system of evaluation must be outlined to measure progress by, for reporting of information to team leaders and members, and a vision of what victory looks like.

Each goal must be celebrated in some fashion. Stop and take a moment and actually build team celebration into the equation so that there is an opportunity for individual recognition of achievement and team recognition of achievement. Learn the team members because reward and recognition on an individual level must be important and add value to the individual. One example is one employee may seek the bonus and another may want an extra day off. A third may want a plaque if significance is their need and others may want tickets to some function. Know your team. Know the individuals. Learn to reward and create certainty for both.

2. The team must have a mission but individuals can have differing visions on how that is to be achieved.

The undertaking of building a team must be mission or objective based. Many people have spoken very effectively on designing with the end objective in mind. I strongly believe in this but the challenge with this in building a team is that when you have the same mission you have several interpretations on how that should be done. Secondly you have each individual with a separate skills and talents and rolls to play in its achievement.

Team players must be reinforced that they support and allow the team to win when they play at their highest level as individuals. If their job is to rebound, let them see the contribution that they make in the team winning. If they are a shooter, many times an open shot is gained when someone sets a screen and allows them to create space for a good shot.

Individuals must be reinforced in the mission or objective to be achieved. Each one should understand this even better than their task or individual role.

Mission keeps each person focused and secure in their position relative to other team members. So each player must be allowed to have separate visions connected to their role to play on how it should be done but not what is to be achieved; same mission, different vision, roles and contributions to make.

3. **The team cannot win without great individual play and great team play. Though an individual may be a great player, the team loses and wins together.**

This is old school. The team does win or lose together. Back to the horrible team I was on that achieved great things individually but never as a team. When the consultants came in they tried what seemed to be a divide a conquer technique where they asked each team member about the other and how the team could approve.

Each member gave a scathing commentary on each other but not enough to have each other removed. Further erosion of the team concept continued until there were not even consistent meetings and no individual interaction between team leaders unless they absolutely had to.

Even staff members began to fight amongst themselves and despise other departments. Interdepartmental recruiting took place to the further detriment of the company.

A truce was called and the consultants finally went away. We could go back to not liking each other in peace. What was decided is that we all had individual roles to play and we made segments among ourselves to work together without threat and reprisal.

We simply met each other's request and required our staffs to go along, get along, and to give the best service to each other as if we were separate companies with customer service in mind. If there was a problem with our staffs, the team leaders would meet and handle it.

The best teams are those who respect each other understand the differing roles to play and are objective based. The great teams find a way to put away their ego for the sake of the team but continue to perform individually at a high level. It's not that they don't have tension; great teams have plenty of tension.

Great teams are self managed and have room for sharp disagreement; they offer differing opinions to for great achievement not for the purpose of disagreement.

4. Great teams have players who accept responsibility for the success of the team.

Quite frankly, if you had a team of individuals who accepts responsibility for themselves, their performances and the success of the team, you will be the best. Great teams that rise above the others and achieve long term dominance like the Lakers, Celtics, Bulls, Patriots etc. all have a few things in common:

Great leadership

Good individual players who become great

Players who play for championships and not stats

Great team chemistry

No individual play above the success of the team

Unselfish players

Long term commitments

Players who manage themselves

5. The individual player must at times defend his place on the court, field, and or space but the player must also be able to score and produce for his team. At times the player must overachieve for his team and do the impossible; they must will the team to victory.

We have all sat on the edge of our seat. Popcorn and drink set aside for the last few moments to determine victory or defeat played out in stadiums and millions of homes. When you give all you have sometimes the team is spent. There is just nothing left. You may the one challenged by the pass having to guard a player bigger than you and if you fail, the team loses.

You could be down by 3 with one last play in overtime and the coach is looking for someone to make the play. If no one steps up and says let me take the last shot and challenges their opponent by shear will then you lose and the championship slips from you hand. No one remembers those in second place.

Business many times is not as glamorous and with few people watching. But the drama in your world is no less dramatic with resources, money and reputations on the line. The greats always find a way to win. Many times when all has been done to win and your team has left everything on the field, great teams become legends when one person finds the will within them to win and overachieves in the moment.

Leaders nurture an atmosphere that encourages people to win and do extraordinary things. Business leaders at times have to coach, cheer, challenge and praise.

6. Balance is the key to consistent winning.

It is true that defense wins games. But in all cases you don't win if you can't score. Teams have to play both great defense and offense. In any project or undertaking there is a time to manage and defend your space on the court. There is also a time for offense and to take risks and develop strategies for the future. There is a time to manage and be creative in the process.

Teams have to first concentrate on getting the right players on the team. It's amazing how the mission becomes so big that no one asks if the team has the right stuff to achieve it.

7. Every day is game day

Great players and teams don't have to get up for game day. If you love what you do and see purpose in your work then you don't need a rivalry to motivate you. Each individual has to have that lunch pale mentality that you came everyday to work and build something great. Remember an investment in the team is an equal investment in you.

I have also been a part of great teams and it feels great to win on game day. Great players don't need external motivation, they know one day that there will be change and they have to be able to look back and have played the game with that school yard mentality that allowed them to play each game as the last. One day it will be over and you will only have the moments that you created, the accolades, and your stories to tell about the big one.

Management Tips:

As you prepare your team take some time and assess the strengths and weaknesses of each member. Engage them in conversation from time to time and find out what motivates them and what rewards they would be interested in receiving from the company.

Consider doing personality profiles on all of your employees to better understand their personalities and motivations.

Look for ways to produce incentives for each employee for both individual rewards for reaching milestones and success as a group.

Chapter 2

Develop an Atmosphere of Authentic Expression

When we decide to live a real authentic expression of which we are and what we decide to do, to become and to live for a destiny greater than our own needs we must get off the fence, move from the fork in the road and choose a path.

A H Fleming, Navigator

Developing an atmosphere of authentic expression or candor is vitally important. I remember one management story (urban legend) about a toothpaste company in a meeting where they were trying to find a way to increase sales after years of sales being flat.

After everyone was finished talking and no one could come up with a good idea, the moderator saw a janitor in the back smiling and shaking his head. The moderator asked him why he was smiling and he said if you want to increase sales, make the hole bigger. This was a multi-million dollar idea.

There is an old saying that if you want to really know what goes on in an organization; ask the guy with the mop. The point is that management does not know everything. Great organizations require feedback at every level.

There are three significant parts to any undertaking that have different input based on their position and their sight from where they are. If you were to climb a mountain at each juncture the view will be different. Base camp in the valley would reveal a daunting task ahead.

Base camp at the mid range to rest for the pursuit ahead would seem different because part of the journey is behind you but the toughest part may lie ahead. The top of the mountain is glorious because if allows you the best vantage point but few make it here. The top not only shows you were you have been and a clearer understanding of the terrain but it shows you new mountains to climb.

The CEO has a vast array of information available to him in a functional organization. His view of things is based on both fact and conjecture.

The managers facts are a little different because much of his information on the daily grind is not shared with the CEO, such minute problems of tardiness, excusing workers to pick up children etc., are not shared in many organizations. The workers view is much different and much more compartmentalized. So who has the clearest view?

The organization that can produce an atmosphere as well as a system of extracting, evaluating, and implementing information from all levels is a healthy organization.

This must go beyond suggestion boxes and meaningless open door policies. CEO and managers must walk the floors and engage workers as well as managers no matter how large the organization. Managers at times must do task work at times to understand the time management and input of the employee in doing his work.

I did a video feature story one time on the Director of a Housing Authority. During the shoot I learned that on scheduled days she dressed up as the maintenance department or other associated departments did and worked as they did.

They were allowed to give her direction and have her due task work. For the filming we had her ride on top of a boom truck and haul garbage from public housing sites.

Her remarks were that she understood and had a much deeper appreciation for their jobs and was able to assess requests for equipment and make critical decisions that affected safety and eventually increased efficiency and productivity.

It is the CEO's job to receive and evaluate information. It is the job of the manager to receive, evaluate and report information. It is the employee's job to produce feedback and information to management that may seem mundane but persistent problems can become critical problems if left unaddressed.

The information pipeline is much like a funnel. It may be wide at the top and continually filtered until it gets to the CEO and Board of Directors but if there is no opportunity to gain new and vital information from the perspective of the people doing the work, then you are not reporting the whole story to the decision makers.

Build an atmosphere where everyone is heard and respected. Not an atmosphere where only some people opinions are honored. Everyone must be honored whether you use his or her ideas or not. Authentic Expression is the highest form of any relationship and a healthy company.

Management Tips:

Go beyond the suggestion box and open door policies.

Walk the floor and spend time managing your employees and building rapport with them.

Let them know that it is okay for them to notify management of problems, legitimate complaints, and how to best make the company better.

Let them know that gossip is never tolerated nor petty innuendo acceptable toward other employees. The purpose of an open management style is for employees to be empowered in improving the work experience and the performance of the company.

Chapter 3
Champion the Cause

Sometimes there is one more fight to prove that we are still champions

A H Fleming

The mission of the company has to become the company mantra from the bottom of the organization to the top. Each task should be recognized as an essential piece to the completion of the mission of the company.

The decisions of finance, operations, marketing, support and fulfillment have to go back to the mission to be achieved. Each decision must be preceded by a question of does this help achieve the mission or does it detract from it.

In working for one organization it became apparent that many decisions to spend money and allocate resources; especially human resources did not seem to have anything to do with what the company mission was.

Many organizations place a lot of energy and time into projects that will not further achieve the stated goals of the company. If the company's goals are not stated then there are too many opportunities for wasted movement, energy, and money.

Stay focused and be sure that the decisions you make help you accomplish the mission of your organization and your team. Its amazing that when employees are empowered to understand that their decisions and performance affect the bottom line, it changes their behavior if they act like and feel like that have a stake in the company. I had a boss one time ask me if you hire this person over the years that is a million dollar decision, would you still hire this person.

I said yes, because hiring that person increased the productivity, which was the right decision in accomplishing the goals of the company many times over what we spent for them. If there was another way remembering the mission would have forced me to re-examine all my alternatives to make sure I made the choice that brought the organization closer to completing its goals.

The company should not only have a mission statement but each employee should know exactly how they contribute to accomplishing it. Having people show up to work because they have to work for a living and not be connected to a larger sense of purpose breads apathy, contempt and lowers productivity.

Get with your employees and find out how many of them know the companies mission statement and the goals of their department or division. If they don't make it an assignment and quiz them until they do. Go further and ask them how they contribute to the success of the company.

Management Tips:

If the company mission statement is not written go through the creative process of writing one.

Post the mission statement as a management goal of achieving it and that all decisions must be driven by the need to accomplish the mission statement.

Continue to build on the mission statement and make it a company mantra, asking management and employees do their behaviour help or hurt the company in accomplishing its goals.

Chapter 4

Trust

Trust me no one knows how they will react until they get hit. So it is in life

A H Fleming

Trust in the work place is very difficult to achieve unless it is a cultivated value that everyone in the organization cherishes and works to achieve. Trust is fragile and what may take a long time to achieve can be easily lost and broken.

Trust must come from the top down and so must the general atmosphere of the company. Trust at the core must be built only on one thing.

Making and keeping promises. Once a promise is made it lives or dies on the integrity in which it was made. *A promise made should be a promise kept.*

Many employees unfortunately come to work with preconceived ideas about the organization and how life in general works. When it comes to trust, trust me people have strong beliefs and feelings about whether or not they can trust management.

Recognizing that some people come to your organization with well worn beliefs and strong feelings of distrust gives you an opportunity to emphasize your core values and the character of the company. If the company generally does not keep its word to its employees, then you have a completely different problem to begin with.

What do you do when trust does not exist or has been broken? Trust is established and re-established the same way. By making and keeping promises. People who have a reason to mistrust must be given a reason to trust again.

The act of building an organization with a foundation of trust will come only from the actions of individuals and management. Trust is built, it may be presupposed in the beginning of any relationship but expectations are easily shattered.

I have had over 20 years of management at the Director to the CEO level. In my years I have had to deal with many employees who came to me with a strong mistrust of management. They just did not expect the company or management to do what they said that they would.

Management must be consistent and transparent. Hidden agendas and personal vendettas have no place in this competitive market where companies are fighting to survive and good and bad management of those companies in many cases makes the difference.

Management Tips:

Post your company's core values, mission statement, and stated goals.

Also state in your policy and procedures manual the companies benefits and rewards.

Put your promises in writing and live up to them.

If you fail to live up to them apologize quickly and move on, be more determined than ever to live up to the promises you make.

When someone has violated the policy and procedures, let the punishment fit crime in the light of what the policies and procedure dictate. Be firm and be consistent.

Be consistent.

Chapter 5

The Power to build or destroy

Positive statements alone without action and a greater understanding that what you're seeking may come but not in the time or way you want it to can destroy hope not build it

A H Fleming

All employees work in an organization. Some employees work to build the vision of the company, some to build their own vision or to further their own agenda. Some come to work seemingly to destroy the organization.

In any case all employees work either builds or undermines the organization. If an employee chooses to follow its leadership, they will follow the leader and not the vision.

Some will follow the vision and not the leader or follow neither the vision nor the leader. Some in rare cases will follow both the leader and the vision; those are the makings of a great organization.

I recently talked to a LPN friend of mine who works in Senior Care. I have managed HUD 202 Senior Facilities so it was interesting talking to her about the intricacies of publicly and privately held facilities and the levels of care.

Time after time the stories always lead back to poor and inconsistent management and employees who did not care about what they were doing and how the projected the success and achievement of the company.

What we don't realize sometimes is that organizations are only expressions of a vision that someone had. Teams of people come together to build that vision and create a tangible interpretation of that dream.

Employees like any segment of the population come to work unhealthy many times both physically and mentally. To not recognize that is irresponsible. Your employees are always your greatest asset. Developing them along with the goods and services that the business provides for monetary exchanges is vitally important.

Each employee has the power to build or slowly undermine and destroy as much of your company as possible. Hiring, motivating, retaining the right employees and getting them to buy into the vision with enthusiasm are important to the survival and growth of your company.

Getting the right people in the organization is the key that will build or destroy your company. Make a concerted strategic effort to get the right people in your organization from the first day to the last. Don't allow wrong people to fester and contaminate a growing organization. It may seem that individuals cannot be easily replaced. The true question is can you afford over the long term to not replace them.

I had a boss one time that was brutal in firing people. Many times it was openly displayed and definitely in violation of many HR policy.

I rarely agreed with the way that he did things but came to agree that firing some people was what needed to be done even when we did not know how we would replace them or in the short term get the job done. Somehow we made it, grew past it and became a better organization for it each time. Get the right people on the bus.

Management Tip:

Spend time really interviewing people and make sure that they speak to someone other than you during the interview process.

Be dedicated to getting the right people in the organization and in the right position. Don't always be quick to fire but when it is obvious, move them to the right position or let them go. Most times you will be doing the organization and them a favor.

Allow people to retain their dignity during the process, it's not personal and make sure that HR policy is followed.

Chapter 6

Work Ethic

Champions do the work that there opponents are not willing to do
                                        A H Fleming

Don't make excuses for your employees. You have to cultivate an atmosphere of discipline and accountability. Work ethic either comes from within because of expectations that were placed on someone in the culture or the way they were raised, some can be motivated using a system of risk and reward but without a great work ethic you cannot build a great company.

Some believe that success is simply a matter of taking advantage of opportunities. Many believe that stars are made overnight. What is rarely seen today is that success mostly comes out of drudgery and hard work. It's the ability to work hard and make short term sacrifices for long term gain that is the true nature of success.

I learned the lesson of hard work not by just doing it but being a part of a team giving it all they got until the work is done. I can share one story with you about a company that I was the Director of Support services.

The company had announced in August that we were relocating to another state and we had to be out by October of that year. This company was over a 60 million dollar a year company with over 400 employees, 4 international offices and offices already in three states. I myself had management support of those international offices and offices in two states.

In the process of who would go and stay with the company none of my staff was asked to go but myself. All of my departments were going to be outsourced by one of the consultants of the company.

I was called upon to transition all of my departments, which were 17 at the time, move the offices and set them up in two other states, renovate the offices in Texas (move location) and sell the warehouse in Orlando that I built, staffed, and managed. What I have not told you yet is that my staff knew that they were being let go and would have to find jobs during the transition.

In Florida we had a small hurricane the week of the move and I can't tell you how difficult it was that week with the rain, motivating staff to pack up and load over 27 tractor trailers going to Texas and California.

When the dust settled and we transitioned each department to outsourcing agents, packed and moved, sold the warehouse and not have a dip in the functions of each department was miraculous. But what I want to focus on was one by one they did what I asked them to do and many left to find jobs when their assignment was done, but there were a faithful few, and even one who stayed with me until the last day when I flew home from California and turned off the lights.

I learned the valuable work ethic of a team that believed in the consistent leadership, strong vision, and fairness that was given to them, they gave me more than I could have ever expected under such an arduous situation.

Take a good hard look at who you have around you and raise the standard higher than it is today and encourage them to strive for excellence and to come within reach of perfection. Let there be no mistakes, work ethic is the way.

Management Tips:

Set a high standard of excellence for your team.

Define your expectations of them before you hire them

I heard someone say that if they can't get fired up with enthusiasm they will be fired with enthusiasm.

You can't instill work ethic, you release it. You give greatness an opportunity; you can produce it in others if they are not looking for an opportunity to be great.

Chapter 7

Owning the Communication Process

The person who owns the communication process is the only one who gets his point across

A H Fleming

We train people how to treat us in every situation. But telling a co-worker or manager that you don't like how you are being treated is not easy.

When you are talking to more than one person about a problem remember that you are not talking to the same person about the problem. Each person must be handled differently. A confrontational style used with one may not get the result you want with the other.

The first thing is to design the conversation around the outcome that you want. Second take into account the person's language, customs, education level etc when addressing them. What may be socially okay for one does not mean it is okay for another.

Third be determined to both own and take responsibility for the conversation. It is your job to make sure they understand what you are trying to say and that you have not been merely heard but understood.

In communication most of the communication process is through physical body language. So in your conversation position yourself to look interested don't overdue hand motions or cross your arms when speaking to someone.

Make sure that in the conversation encourage questions and ask people to parrot back to you what they heard you say. This will let you know if they understood you and it gives you an opportunity to say it differently. Be quick to listen and slow to speak.

Become a master communicator, be clear in your body language, tone, and choose your words carefully. Don't talk down to people or pontificate uselessly to impress others.

Remember being understood is the goal, not to impress or demagogue. Study communication and how people react in situations where someone may be aggressive or have their feelings hurt. Take the extra time to make sure that you have communicated well and been understood.

Management Tips:

Study communication and become a master communicator

Speak clearly and choose your words based on a predetermined outcome

Don't communicate serious issues through email. Remember much of the communication process is left out and it's up to the individual to interpret HOW you said something, which changes the meaning.

Remember that all people are not the same. Change your communication styles to fit the situation.

Encourage questions and have people parrot back to you what was said.

Chapter 8

Choose Your Battles

Before you fight to win; you must choose to fight
                                                    A H Fleming

Choose your battles. Don't be thin skinned. Not every issue needs to be dealt with through confrontation. Sometimes you have to let it go and move one as long as someone else's bad behavior is not a pattern.

Not every battle is strategic to winning the war. Even when an issue needs to be addressed, it should always be addressed in the context of you are trying to achieve through the conversation. Avoiding a fight that is not strategic to winning should not be considered a loss.

Which battles should be fought? Battles only associated with changing the long-term outcomes, policy or procedural items that could affect the health of the company, or battles that challenge your authority in a way where you could be discredited.

Battles over meaningless things that are outwardly insignificant should be carefully weighed before war is waged.

Sometimes you can win small battles but lose your objectivity and loose the war in the process of trying to be right or in control. Further small skirmishes only deplete your resources and expend emotional energy.

Management Tips:

*Know yourself and be aware of your feelings
and the benefit you perceive you get when you
react a certain way.*

*Choose your battles and if it is not strategic
take the high ground.*

*Don't be defensive, be offensive in nature, be
focused on taking new ground.*

*Don't stop what you are doing to answer the
critics when your work and reputation and
speak for themselves.*

Chapter 9

No Place for the Ego

The ego must be well formed in order to give it up; but the process of giving it up is required to build a great organization beyond your time of leadership

A H Fleming

I used to think that every leader has to have a certain amount of ego delicately balanced against humility and transparency. I have since learned through my own experience and watching various leaders of companies that there is no place for ego at work.

Ego is the part of us that sees ourselves separate from everyone and everything; that our needs are more important than the needs of others or the organization.

Ego driven people are soon discovered to have strong agendas and only for their own advancement and significance. They live for their own kingdom and don't usually put succession plans in place or train people to take their place when their gone.

The more you can build confidence in yourself and those whom you lead without the self serving need to be right, be heard, or to be in control, the better off your organization will be. A great organization does not start to be great until it can divorce itself from ego or personality lead leaders.

No matter the product or service no organization will be great over the long run being choked out by egomaniacs. In Ego's world there is nothing larger than self and nothing more important. There is no place for oversized egos in enduring great organizations.

Management Tips:

Know yourself and make sure that you don't perform for significance and you don't require others to do the same.

Allow yourself and others to be significant and appreciated for the work they do, how they do it and the results they achieve without acting out for attention and respect or just to be heard or seen.

Chapter 10
Pick up the paper

Don't ask someone else to do what you are not willing to do. Walking over paper exposes your diminished attitude toward yourself and others

A H Fleming

The mark of any great organization is when everyone is willing to pick up the paper. As I walked into an employee's office I noticed some paper had fallen on the ground. I wondered how long it was there, though the employee was busy did others walk over it, did they not pick it up?

What example would I have set if I walked by and did not pick it up? Though there was no fanfare, balloons or trumpets, I believe that when everyone is willing to do the small things the great things get that much easier to do together. Build trust, set an example and being willing to pick up the paper.

I was watching a nightly news show one time and they were talking about Wal-mart. I don't remember the ladies name but she was one of the senior managers who had worked her way up from an hourly position in one of the smaller departments. She talked about the details of which Wal-Mart runs their operations and no detail is overlooked in reporting and trying to find solutions.

The smallest thing they showed in the story but brought her point home to me was as she was walking in the door she stopped and cleaned up paper around the trash can in the front door area. That is the kind of caring and attention to detail that makes Wal-Mart a strong company.

Management tips:

Pay attention to the details

Showing that you care about your job is not always in the big decisions that get a lot of attention but shown in the small things that are done without fanfare.

Pick up the paper

Chapter 11

Never have to look over your shoulder

Truth is the ultimate mirror in which no one is afraid to look when you have been truthful

A H Fleming

Everyone in the company especially the management should walk in integrity to where they should not have to look over their shoulder and where each decision made can stand on its own merits.

My goal for a period of time was to work and manage in such a way that I never had to apologize. It's not because I thought I was too good or that in some circumstances it was not necessary to foster good relationships but I tried to walk in such integrity that I did not have to.

The first principle is that if you walk in absolute integrity, **not perfection**, then you don't have to worry about the decisions you make. If you have made an honest mistake and it was wrong then the company protocol will take care of how it is addressed but your character and integrity stay intact.

Usually if an honest mistake was made to accomplish the companies' vision, typically management may critique your decision and point out where it could have been done differently but you should be able to maintain their trust and respect. If they fire people for honest mistakes then you may need to find another place of employment anyway.

Second when you scrutinized and it is found that you stole money or used a situation for personal gain, you may have gained in the short term but will loose big in the long run. There is no bigger loss than the erosion of character.

Management tips:

Walk in integrity and excellence. Keep good records of transactions and decisions that are made. If you make a mistake own up to it and give good and bad information to superiors equally.

Let your goal in management be excellence and not perfection.

Perfection over a long period of time is not obtainable and though the pursuit may be a lofty goal, it will lead to only condemnation and frustration. Mistakes are a learning process and should be viewed as presenting new opportunities to make things work properly.

Chapter 12

Don't live for the Shoe box

At the end of the day if what you leave with is not larger than the shoe box, you have failed to realize character and honor cannot be contained; it's infectious

A H Fleming

This is a concept that teaches to not make day-to-day decisions based on outward rewards only.

Not that money and recognition are not good rewards but when they are the only rewards in which an individual defines their self worth, then that person is in trouble when those accolades are not given or worse when at the end of a career the person can fit their worth in a shoe box.

The first major position that I held and it would not be the last where the company moved or I was let go as Chief Executive Officer. Each time

I remember my last day as if it was yesterday. On all my jobs I was able to walk away with my relationships and honor because of the decisions that I made and the way I carried myself. But I never walked away with anything that I could not fit in a shoe box.

We have to live for internal integration rather than external things that make us feel significance. If we live for the external than we have learned nothing and add nothing of value to our journey.

Business should be run based on vision and values. I counsel people all the time and tell them to live their lives and make business decisions on the larger picture and not the flavor of the moment, don't try to find significance in material things that bring only temporary happiness.

Management tips:

Manage in such a way that if it was your last day you would have developed yourself, developed others, and found great meaning and significance in your work and relationships.

Don't live for material gain and accolades. Both fade over time but only lasting memories, life lessons, and relationships remain.

Chapter 13

Suspend your skepticism

The critic and the skeptic are neighbors; avoid them both

A H Fleming

The benefit of the doubt; its easily given and violated most of the time. However, you still have to be able to extend some trust, especially to your team until they violate that trust. Good managers do manage information but what's more important is how they manage themselves first, then others.

Build an atmosphere of trust by allowing there to be a way to win both for the company, management, and the employee. Many feel that no matter what they do they can't win. In my own journey where I had multiple departments and responsibilities, I found that the less time I spent managing tasks and not employees, the more problems that I had.

The opposite is true and profound. Manage people and most of the problems go away.

It's also important to be able to restore people once they have made a mistake. Being able to suspend your skepticism is important because you have to make the other person feel that you can trust them again.

If it's an offense that is too great to restore trust or it could cause a liability to the company then they should be let go, but with dignity.

Suspend your skepticism and value judgment in order to build trust. Suspend your judgment and let their character and consistency of action define them. You will see that this will define you as well.

Management tips:

Don't be skeptical and critical.

Make sure that employees understand your expectations not just the rules, policies, and operational procedures.

Build an atmosphere of trust

Take time to manage your employees and not just tasks

Be a master communicator

Chapter 14

Where Are We?

You know where you are; you either have disconnected from the destination or you are afraid to here the truth

A H Fleming

Many times in any venture we lose touch on where we are at the moment relative to the end result we desire. Sometimes we get so entrenched in the day-to-day problems that we lose sight of the end goal all together. What if there is no end goal, and the daily dissatisfaction in your work is all there is?

In life and business we have to create anchors. Anchors are things that we have set in place that no matter the weather, whether it's storming or placid we are tied to something that keeps us internally still. Anchors prove what we already believe.

Many times when I seem to lose my bearing I go back and read my core values, personal mission statement, and my annually desired outcomes. I don't change my core values at all, with extreme trepidation review my mission statement for change and very seldom change my annual desired outcomes.

So it must be for business. The day-to-day grind can make all of us loose our place relative to the desired end results. Without anchors and other things in our life whether prayer, rituals, milestones etc., we can lose all bearing and sense of purpose and even worse our sense of value.

The anchor is merely something to evaluate your position against so that you realize that you are not drifting off course. If you have merely coarse correct and make the adjustments necessary.

When I go back and read my anchors they set me back in place and help me get my bearing. Since I don't draw my identity by merely what I do, then my personal value is not affected by a bad day at work, mistake, or an act prompted by a lack of judgment. In life sometimes you have to take the time to weigh anchor.

Management tips:

Make sure your personal and company mission statement is written and reviewed by yourself and the employees

From time to time take time out and push away from the table and reconnect to your sense of purpose and self definition to center you and get you back on track.

Chapter 15

Am I?

Don't ask me who you are; ask the liar in the mirror

A H Fleming

Many times I have had people ask me who am I? The *am I* could be anything; what they are really looking for is validation. The last time someone asked me that was "am I insecure"?

I asked them why they asked me and what was the outcome of this conversation that they wanted? They assured me that they trusted me and wanted to know what I thought.

Without thinking I told them what did it matter what I thought. I asked them were they insecure and after beating around the bush for 5 minutes they said no. Than if you define yourself as not being insecure than it matters not what I think.

I did tell them to honestly evaluate their life both where they are strong and weak and don't rely on their strengths nor grieve their weaknesses. Work on them and adjust the list periodically to what is a true reflection of you. Getting to know yourself and self-definition is the greatest gift that I could give her.

This will help with your evaluations and interactions with employees as well in your business. The question of Am I is personal but spills over into your business? It's the process of evaluation and definition.

In order to evaluate your gain an answer your mind asks a question. How you answer that question either leads to more questions, a correct or an incorrect answer. This answer will affect the behavior of the individual or the company as a whole. This is the power of the question.

Management tips:

A company will discover itself in its journey if it has no vision to become.

It will only become great by asking great questions, large by asking large questions of it that it requires answers to.

Learn the power of the question and how to get answers.

Don't be afraid to ask

Chapter 16

Don't cry when it rains

I always say that good times and bad times don't last always. The unsafe place is in the middle of the road but it's where you have to be from time to time to get that adrenaline rush

A H Fleming

There is a scripture that says it rains on the just and the unjust. In other words everybody gets wet sooner or later. To cry when it rains is to only look at rain as a negative that happens to us without any thought to the benefit of the rain.

Sure, rain can be inconvenient and change the best-laid plans. If too much rain occurs in a short period of time it can be catastrophic.

But many times in our lives the daily shower, with some lightning and thunder is merely a temporary problem causing the normal traffic jams and messy hair.

Rain however, does allow us to grow and many times in the workplace when it rains it can be a sign of things changing. I see rainy days and merely part of the cycle of life, the necessary thing to cause some things to grow as well as expose the weaknesses of some of the things we structure in our life.

When it rains on the job it may be a sign that your values and those values of your boss or workplace no longer complement each other and there is a leak or worse flooding.

Rain could also be a sign of life, opening up discussions and events that might not have taken place unless the status quo was interrupted.

But a healthy environment is structured well to anticipate the rain. Rain can be viewed as a good thing bringing life and exposing the cracks or a negative thing that when tested floods and destroys the landscape. Understand your terrain and always take the high ground.

Don't cry when it rains, because it will rain sooner or later. Your energy would best be spent building your house on values that are not easily shaken or moved.

Would you rather live in the desert or a rain forest or somewhere in between? It's up to you.

Management tips:

Don't cry when it rains. Take stock of the damage if any. How you define the experience is critical. The same thing that exposes problems also brings life.

Look at things positively and they will be positive.

Take the opportunity for deeper discussion, reflection, and change.

Chapter 17

Cold filtered is
not always smooth!

Living with filters on or blinders never gets you the truth

A H Fleming

As you grow in years of management, one of the biggest problems with technology is that it can ruin our communication.

Most of the communication process is body language, words, and voice inflections. Email and other forms of technology don't allow for how something is said past the words that are used.

So much of the process is missing and we have to interpret how something was said to get the full meaning and there lies the room for mistakes on what was actually meant by the words that we used.

Cold filtered is not always smooth means that when you get information from anyone especially those who are loyal and those who are disloyal to you remember that the information is always filtered, spun, changed and sometimes just plain old wrong.

Also when viewing information such as emails that are incomplete there is a lot of room for misinterpretation or mistakes.

Many times I have had information passed on to me that was said in a way that was not in the original tone or meaning of the person who sent the message. By the time I went to confront the person I was in full attack mode.

You have to teach your assistants and employees not to filter and or spin information given to them. Tell them to tell it like it is or in this case like it was. Before you re-act give the other person the benefit of the doubt and go to them to first understand and then to be understood.

You also have to train yourself not to react to emails but be willing to ask people what they meant by what was sent to you.

Management Tips:

Train your assistants and employees not to filter information. Make sure that in communicating information they don't have their own agenda being added to the information.

Ask questions about information that is communicated in a way that does not allow for you to determine how something was said.

Chapter 18

Politics

No vote, no voice. Politics sucks but through it the few control the many

A H Fleming

Politics is a dirty word in the work place. It is both loathed and used in the work place to secure additional money, status, time off and a myriad of perks.

I define politics as the struggle for power. The fact of the matter is that by what means you gain power, status and other things is the same matter by which it can be taken away.

Leadership is an earned position of service to the company and people. Authority is given because trust has been established. Authority that is taken can be taken away.

Politics is and always will be a matter of values and beliefs. Sometimes politics can create conflicting beliefs or confusion. I personally don't consciously practice politics in the work place. Because I don't define myself by outward things, I don't feel need to drive the right car, do the right lunch or struggle for power because I don't feel the need to possess position and or status.

I work from a place of character and defined values none of which are to achieve anything outside of planning, strategy, and hard work. Therefore the things earned are not easily taken away because there were not given on superficial things. Office politics can be cruel and in the end your character and achievement matter more than position and even money.

Management Tips:

Be wary of playing office politics. Anything given can be taken away, only things that are earned are enduring.

Lead by character and your integrity to live up to the values that you hold for yourself and those who work for you. Don't go with the flow because it's easier to swim. Sometimes swimming against the current is what guarantees your survival.

Chapter 19

Surviving the Consultant

Those that can't teach; those who have done and failed consult

A H Fleming

I write this chapter with a little humor because I have been a business and real estate development consultant myself. I have been one and I have survived them.

I am always aware of how much help any organization needs in strategically planning its growth, expansion of its markets etc. I am also aware that the influence can be one of empowerment and significant change to an organization.

It can also mean a waste of money, moral killer, and genuine upheaval throughout the entire organization.

The consultant dynamic is one where the consultant and management have to not just look at the bottom line but the human dynamic at all times.

Change is difficult and so is criticism but it is even harder to take from someone from the outside. By bringing in a consultant you are sending a perceived message to the staff that they are inferior or need help because they could not get it done.

You could also send a message to the staff the extra help has arrived and seek to always produce a culture that is based on hiring when necessary but bringing extra help through outsourcing so that consultants and contractors are not threatened by this new dog marking his territory on the copier.

To survive the consultant is more than just spin. You have to have clear parameters and reasons why the consultant is there. Don't make the consultant the end all and be all too all the company's problems but do play to their strengths, experience, and expertise.

Go the extra mile and reassure the employees that the consultant is there to serve them and bring solutions that in the long term make their job easier and the company stronger. Remember to manage relationships and not just problems.

Management Tips:

Clearly define the scope of work for the consultant.

Make sure that the consults role is one of service and non-threatening to the employees and management.

Thank the employees as well as the consultant for working together and producing a good product.

Don't ever disclose what the consultant is getting paid.

Chapter 20

Be Consistent

Consistency makes the experience known before it's experienced

A H Fleming

If I could think of one thing that will make you successful or a failure, just one common denominator, it would be consistency of doing things either right or wrong, either in line with or opposition to your values or the thing that needs to be achieved.

Being consistent means that you do things by design, with purpose and they are done the same way over and over again so that others around you can depend on you.

Inconsistency in an organization breeds mistrust and imbalance because employees never know where they stand or what to expect.

The key is to look at the systems and take most of the judgment calls out of making decisions. If you are always winging it at work and making it up as you go then your company is lacking good operational procedures.

Take the time to put them in place; good systems will make an organization much more profitable over the long term.

Management Tips:

> *Review your operational policies and amend them as needed; it should be a living document.*
>
> *Remember that some decisions set precedent.*
>
> *Making inconsistent decisions breed mistrust.*
>
> *Don't interpret policy to fit your circumstances. If the policy is wrong work to change it.*

Chapter 21

Strategy does not always win the war

Strategy without adaptation and change is merely dogma; or dog stuff

A H Fleming

Developing a strategy goes a long way to preparing your staff to achieve your companies goals. But strategy does not always win the war.

Being able to make decision based on current evaluations of the situation, up to date information about what is happening on the battle field is more than important, it's critical.

If you are a student of conflict or war, you see many times that certain mistakes were made because relevant information was not available or poor decisions were made based on wrong evaluations, weak character and lack of will to succeed. Some of these decisions would have changed the course of history.

So where does strategy fit into the equation of a successful undertaking? Developing a good strategy is vital to getting started with the greatest impact with putting forth the least amount of effort. Strategy has to be continually re-evaluated and re-visited.

Strategy becomes obsolete and outdated the minute you begin any undertaking. Constant change and evaluation of the market, competition, and internal processes are critical to you company making changes that keep you relevant.

What must strategy be in order to offer any insight and strength to the endeavor?

Disciplined

Firm

Direct

Concise

Evaluated

Changed

Evaluated

Changed

Evaluated

Changed

Etc.

Management Tips:

Review your strategy in operations, finance, product development etc.

Make sure that you have a system that works in getting information from the market as well as the employees and vendors. This is critical to staying relevant.

Develop a planning team to make the present more efficient and the future strategy that focuses on keeping the company relevant and competitive.

Chapter 22

True Wealth is in the Assets

If you own land and lose everything else you can still live on your land in a tent

A H Fleming

So much of life really could come down to basic rules of investment. Not necessarily buy low and sell high but there are times when that is appropriate and it works to a company's profit.

The true wealth in a leader and creator is to see the true wealth in something that someone else cannot see and bring it out.

I remember a story about the creation of Michael Angelo's David. Someone asked how he created such a beautiful piece of art from only one piece of marble. His reply was that David was always in there, he just chipped away the excess.

I also have read about Donald Trump and it seems to me that his real gift is being able to see something special in real estate that no one else could see. He invested himself more than the money until the vision he saw was reality. He made money because he bet that others would see it too and be willing to pay premium prices for the experience of the "Trump Touch".

Our wealth is really based on the assets in we are able to develop and retain. Cash flow is important but not the basis of creating long term wealth unless it is saved managed and invested.

Debatable but I think the greatest asset of a corporation is its intellectual property, this vast untapped resource in its people and you. This is where largest amount of potential wealth lies.

Management Tips:

Build your employees and offer them opportunities to grow in their jobs and as individuals.

Don't just direct employees manage them and give them opportunities for real growth. Show them how they contribute to the bottom line and how what they do has purpose.

Show them that they are valuable.

Encourage creative thinking and be solutions driven. The next million could come from an idea from someone in any area of the company.

Chapter 23

Learn to laugh out loud

I never want to work for a company where I don't have to leave my office to find out what's so funny

A H Fleming

Joy is infectious, much the same way that laughter is. The dream of most managers and employees is to simple enjoy the work they do for a living but so often we hear about that such a large percentage don't.

It's okay to laugh and an occasionally a good gut busting laugh should be okay, not necessarily the kind of laugh that would get you kicked out of church, but a real infectious laugh that lets you know that people enjoy their work and hopefully each other.

Synergy is created when people of like values and with a common purpose come together, but when people don't enjoy what they do, productivity goes down, and sick days go up. Learn to laugh out loud and allow an atmosphere to develop where others can laugh along with you.

You don't create laughter you just let it go!

Management Tips:

Take the work seriously, not yourself sometimes.

While a work atmosphere is appropriate allow room for infectious joy to break out, people who laugh are usually healthier and more productive.

Chapter 24

Position the Plow

Don't do a beaver's job without the teeth to do it

A H Fleming

I was reminded recently that some things that seem easy from a certain position may not be easy at all. Sometime in management we don't fully understand the scope of each position we manage unless we have done the work ourselves.

A friend who grew up in Puerto Rico on a farm on what would be considered by today's standards meager beginnings shared with me a story from her childhood.

Her father was plowing the field one day and he asked her to take the reins of the ox and walk behind them and guide the plow while he worked the oxen up front by guiding them.

Some time went by and her position was always that of walking behind the oxen and guiding this heavy plow. Now for a young female on a farm, she often resented the hard work while her friends were playing and being kids. What made matters worse is to watch her father take the easiest job of walking the oxen and guiding them.

One day as they went out to plow the field, her father asked her why she was upset. She told him that she was doing all the hard work while he guided the ox. He asked her, which do you think is the harder job; to be in front or behind the ox. She quickly answered that she had the harder job.

So he switched positions and put her in front of the ox, charging her with controlling the huge beasts through the fields. She quickly learned that working them from the front position was not as easy as she had thought and saw the process from a different position that gave her an instant appreciation for what he part of the task was.

In management sometimes the employees as well as we don't have a clear perspective on the importance of each role. We shouldn't but many times we take the jobs of other for granted by not fully understanding what is like to do their jobs.

Take time to understand what it is your employees have to do on a daily basis and don't take it for granted. Sometimes jobs that are monotonous are the hardest to do, as they are repetitious and repeat the same tasks over and over. Appreciate each job and understand its place in the big picture.

Management Tips:

Make sure you have a job description for each position.

Go beyond the job description and have them write down what they really do, many times the two are not that close.

Take some time out once a week or month and do the job of some of your employees. Take complaint calls and actually deal with the stress of their job and get a deeper appreciation for what they do.

Chapter 25

The Death of Optimism

I believe we will be free; just not by Christmas

A H Fleming

Don't take this as a statement that to be optimistic is wrong. I believe strongly that you have to be passionate, enthusiastic about your core beliefs and when challenged optimistic.

The death of the type of optimism that is usually connected to blind faith at times needs to die because it has no place in the lives of most truly successful people. Let me give you a definition of what I am talking about.

Optimism is much like hope that only endures if one can escape the crisis that you are in without any rational understanding of why your circumstance may change, by what means, and how do you maintain and even prosper in the midst of great crisis.

Optimism should be engaged with planning and a resounding statement of faith that no matter how long it takes we are going to accomplish our objective.

Optimism without planning leaves your circumstances to just hoping that something will change without planning and acting as if it will. Optimism without real reason is just wishful thinking. Optimism with planning and action is expressed faith in a certain outcome.

Be optimistic, if you define what you what, plan and act then you have a reason to feel like you will accomplish it.

Management Tips:

Be enthusiastic

Define what it is you want to accomplish or experience in writing

Read it on a regular basis

Plan for it, act to get it, and act as if it is going to happen

Chapter 26

Iron sharpens Iron

My enemy is my friend; our battles make me a better warrior

A H Fleming

Many times I have asked to sit in on a complaint session as if I was only there to side with the person who is doing the complaining.

After such complaining sessions and threats to quit or do bodily harm to their supervisors or other employees, I would analyze what was said and then ask them some simple questions.

What did you learn from this situation?
How do you think you are changing through this situation?

On and on my questions become more piercing, not to agree with them but to get them to confront themselves about how they are being changed in the process. Many times we don't see opposing situations and people as our teachers.

Crisis reveals character. I have heard this said many times and in different ways but it is true that crisis reveals what is inside or us, it weighs and measures us. It also gives us an opportunity to change. The pressure of situations squeezes us and what is in us comes out, sometimes with frightening voracity.

Iron is sharpened by iron. It may be that hard situations have to be used on a hard head but life has a way of using situations that are harder than us to sharpen us and change us. When we are pliable we can change more easily, when we are hard, or just plain hard headed we can break.

Management tips:

Realize that situations are either created by us or even if they are not and come into our life as a form of crises if we internalize them then we can be affected and most times in a negative way. They can appear to further our negative and limiting belief systems.

Crisis can also be viewed as an opportunity to overcome and sharpen your skills.

In crisis we are changed but we are either changing for the good or reinforcing our negative beliefs.

Help your employees see that any situation can be handled in a number of different ways but it can be a teaching tool that can improve their resolve and skills.

Chapter 27

The Champions Gate
(Taken from the book "Its Your Fight to Win")

"One who is samurai must, before all things, keep constantly in mind, by day and by night....that he has to die".

Daidoji Yuzan (16th Century)

The Champions Gate is the place of entrance into a new life of excellence, peace, and service. Entering through the gates means a literal death to some of the limiting beliefs and corresponding actions that are keeping from achieving the absolute potential for which you were created.

The Champions Gate is the point of entry into a new beginning of discipline, connection, and purpose. My Champions Gate was through a personal relationship with God, defining my life's purpose, discipline of the martial arts, and working toward a life of excellence daily.

In any city or stronghold there are entrances, in some cases merely gates that you enter through to go inside other are highways in which you enter and leave.

In many cultures still practiced today there is an expectation of what is to be thought of you as a man or women, a right of passage expected of you to reach and to walk through with all of its mysteries on the other side. If you join a group or fraternity there is a process by which you are screened, taught the rules and initiated into something larger than yourself.

On the other side there is more than a sense of belonging, there is forever a brand, a name, and association in which you are a part of. This can be either good or bad.

If you are a felon than you are forever reminded of belonging to that group. You have to work hard and move on from your past and enter through another gate to be a part of another more worthy group.

As I think about this word warrior I think that there must be a price of admission. I remember I was in an office one day when the subject came up about a group of guys wanting to fight me. They had heard that I could fight and they wanted to try me. I guess they thought I would back down or suggest peace as being a better way. I told them that I would not hurt them and would be glad to teach them in the way. My Sensei who was there talked them about training and how well I could fight. They soon declined my invitation and decided not to walk through that gate or even understand the price of admission.

In that group there was one person left. He was a relatively quiet person but in talking with him he like to take short cuts with work and with business ventures and always was looking for an angle not to do the hard work or do things right. He had asked to train with me, he was intrigued about the martial arts and wanted to learn.

I did not think he would make a good candidate as our training was not based on belts but on the knowledge of self and the discipline of the art. I thought though maybe he could use the lessons that are taught there and maybe it would make him a better person. I watched Sensei speak to him and just flatly deny him that he would teach him. I agreed but was puzzled by this. I later learned that character and not just motivation it is the

Champions Gate. A man or woman must be a person of character in order to become something greater. The person asking was not. He was weak not by circumstance but by choice. At your very core, what you are is what you are in secret when the lights are out and when no one else is around. Character is the essence of who and what we are.

Everyone must enter life and must leave it. From spirit we have come and back to it we must go. From the dust of the earth our bodies have come and from it, it shall return. Everything in life must enter by some gate and enter into another.

What we do between the gates of entering and leaving is what counts and echoes into eternity. Sensei would not train this man because of his character could not be trained. He was not teachable. There are no shortcuts to greatness and no means of manipulation that man can become something other than what he is.

"The Champions Gate is a man's character. By it he will enter and leave each circumstance. It will lead him to honour and riches or destruction. Our character left unchecked will choose for us"

Ayub Fleming

We are always in constant state of change. But in life there are constants. Character is one of them. If a man does not discipline himself much like the master swordsman heats and beats the sword to perfect it, than we are doomed to the benefits of our own nature. We are and we are becoming.

It is said that many want to change their circumstance and not their character. It will not work. If a great fighter in any sport disciplines himself but still cheats to overcome his opponent, it will sooner or later only lead him to shame and dishonour.

I have many great men in my life and many though despite their talents could never achieve any significance. I have almost always seen the difference as a matter of character. So many great actors, athletes, and entertainers have done so many great things but some have come crashing down due to lack of character.

Character is simply shaped by values and your ability to live up to those values on a day-to-day basis. Winning in the small victories when you are not seen, no crowds to cheer you on to the larger victories.

Character is moulded and shaped; it is exposed to the heat of trial after trial and prevails in the will. It is the Champions Gate.

Management Tips:

Character is the Champions gate. Decide now who you are going to be and how you are going to live your life and by what values you are going to live by.

Write down your core values and hold yourself to them.

Motivate yourself to live by them by thinking about the consequences of being the person you have designed. How does honour feel, success, honesty and how does it feel to life, cheat or steal.

Become a shaped vessel of honour. Each small victory forges your character to be the strength you need to climb higher mountains.

"In strategy your spiritual bearing must not be any different from normal. Both in fighting and in everyday life you should be determined though calm. Meet the situation without tenseness yet not recklessly, your spirit settled yet unbiased.

If the enemy thinks of the mountains, attack like the sea; and if he thinks of the sea, attack like the mountains".

Miyamoto Musashi (1584-1645)

Chapter 28

It's Your Fight to Win or Loose

"It takes a lot of courage to develop an authentic expression of yourself and to put yourself out there and live your dreams. To face down opposition and personal problems and continue to fight even when everyone and everything is telling you give up; you can't win.

What's funny is when you are knocked out and come to; you are the one telling yourself not to get up. The voice you hear sometimes is your own.

Make no mistake this is your life and you have to contend for it. This is the fight of your life, the only shot you have to be champion, to master your life and reach its full potential. Winning and losing feel very differently in the end and so is the preparation that gets you close to winning or losing".

"It's Your fight to Win" **Ayub Fleming**

In business and life we face tough opposition. There are always competing forces around us that test the very metal we are made of. In some extreme cases they challenge our right to expression; even our very survival. In business you have to be tough and at times to seem ruthless but without lowering your standards or losing your character.

Developing a warrior spirit and a tribal unity in your business is critical. Sometimes people work but have no sense of belonging or purpose. You have to get the right people in training camp to solidify your team. If you have the wrong people you will know it when you face your opposition. Your team won't be focused or prepared but your opponent will.

It's your fight to win, so develop the right team, prepare, train, and get ready for the opposition because in business everyday is game day.

Management tips:

Make sure that each employee belongs and contributes to the bottom line

Make sure the mission is stated and becomes a tribal mantra, if some want to go to another tribe help them pack. As a team you win or loose.

Develop a warrior spirit based on purpose and resolute to live with honor and compassion.

Chapter 29

Good and Bad Times
Don't Last Always

Every day is either good or bad depending on your reaction and definition and not the events of the day

A H Fleming

I can't tell you how many times I have used this line to get people through the moment as well as myself at times of being overwhelmed by the circumstances. When we are faced with tough times and tougher situations it is good to remember that good and bad times don't last always.

Life has this ebb and flow to it that when things are good, save for a rainy day. When things are bad, analyze and make plans and preparations to outlast the famine and expand into the future.

We have to learn from all situations that we are in and act from a deeper place of character. I can't stress this enough because I have seen people act completely differently in business depending on whether or not cash flow was good or their stock fell 100 points by lunch.

In business and our personal life, two things we need at all times are balance and perspective. Balance is our ability to manage the things on two extremes not in the middle. You have to not just be able to play the middle of the road; you must be able to balance people of situations in the extreme.

I have often said that truth is not found by the centrist but by those who are patient enough to listen to people from extreme points of view. It takes constant feedback and minor adjustments to keep things in balance.

Perspective allow us to see the things closest to us but never forgetting that change will come and that if we stay the course set and again make minor adjustments we can reach our destination. When you laugh don't laugh too long or hard, change will come.

When things are no laughing matter remember the times when you could and realize that they will come again. When things are bad and all that you are is challenged, remember that you have a plan, stick to it or adjust it but don't abandon it. Good and bad times don't last always.

Management tips:

Live life from the middle understanding that both good and bad times take minor adjustments to keep things balanced.

Balance is the ability to control extremes not to mask changes but manage it.

In the good times rejoice and save

In the bad times remember, and know that good times will return.

Stick to your plan, evaluate and adjust.

Chapter 30

Position vs. Influence

Position is only power until you lose it; Influencers are followed wherever they go

A H Fleming

In one position where I was a director over several departments, I had a supervisor who only was there for about 3 weeks. His name was Blackburn. I remember he was a stern man, tall and in good shape, which he appeared to be well seasoned in his business accomplishments.

I remember he would sternly tell you to get in his office right now and bring this or that report. I had most of his duties when he came in so he expected me to be his biggest problem.

I did what he asked and listened to one tirade after another and all his grandiose plans of developing his kingdom. He had authority and he meant on using it to the fullest.

One time he called me into his office, demanding that I bring this report and when I got there he started to tell me about some of his plans and who was a problem for him. I guess he thought at this time after two weeks I was no longer a threat.

After listening to him a while, I leaned over his desk and told him that he did not want to do what he said and that sooner or later the owner was going to go to the people that he saw as his opposition and ask them what they thought about the new tyrant. Sooner or later he would be out.

He told me I was wrong and that he was going to do this or that. I soon left his office and shook my head. I could not believe that after all his degrees and business accomplishments that he has not learned one of the most basic lessons.

Influence in stronger than position.

Always has been and always will be. The person with position is not always the person who has the boss's ear. The person who has their confidence is really the person with the most power.

It's why people are circumvented and others asked to do tasks that were theirs to do and on and on. Sooner or later the boss is going to ask someone else about you and what they say may have a lot of influence on your future.

One morning about 5:30a I was in my office doing PO's and I looked up and he was coming into my office with no tie on but dressed in business casual. I knew he was coming to fire me so I greeted him and prepared for the worse.

He sat down and told me that the boss did ask someone else and decided to let him go. He told me that he thought I would be his biggest problem but ended up being his only support.

Live by purpose and seek to be influential not to be powerful because of position. Influence is the true position of power.

Management tips:

Don't manage by gimmicks you read out of a magazine.

Manage by character and honor

Seek to be influential and not just powerful through position

Live in truth so that you don't have to worry about what you say or do

Thank you for purchasing this and other Living the Max Life materials. We are glad that you have decided to invest in your personal development.

For more information on this and other inspirational resources go to www.ahfleming.com.